Abraham Lincoln

AN EXTRAORDINARY LIFE

I0973297

Abraham Lincoln

AN EXTRAORDINARY LIFE

Harry R. Rubenstein

Published in Association with the National Museum of American History
Kenneth E. Behring Center

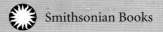 Smithsonian Books

This book accompanies the Smithsonian National Museum of American History's exhibition *Abraham Lincoln: An Extraordinary Life*. This exhibition was made possible by the generous support of:

FORD MOTOR COMPANY FUND
RICHARD LOUNSBERY FOUNDATION
HISTORY CHANNEL

Photographer credits: Michael Barnes, Harold Dorwin, John Elder, Larry Gates, Hugh Talman, Eric Long, Terry McCrae, Richard Strauss, and Ricardo Vargas.

Edited by Christina Wiginton
Designed by Jody Billert / Design Literate, Inc.

Library of Congress Cataloging-in-Publication Data
Rubenstein, Harry R., 1951-
Abraham Lincoln : an extraordinary life / [Harry R. Rubenstein]. — 1st ed.
p. cm.
"Accompanies the Smithsonian National Museum of American History's exhibition
Abraham Lincoln : an extraordinary life"—T.p. verso.
Includes bibliographical references.
ISBN 978-1-58834-263-8 (pbk.)
1. Lincoln, Abraham, 1809-1865—Exhibitions. 2. Lincoln, Abraham, 1809-1865—Anniversaries, etc.—Exhibitions.
3. Presidents—United States—Biography—Exhibitions. 4. National Museum of American History (U.S.)—Exhibitions.
I. National Museum of American History (U.S.) II. Title.
E457.65.R83 2008
973.7092—dc22
2008032772

First Edition

14 13 12 11 10 09   5 4 3 2

ISBN 978-1-58834-263-8

Printed in China

PREVIOUS SPREAD:
President Abraham Lincoln, 1862

LINCOLN IN RICHMOND
On April 4, 1865, Lincoln made a triumphant visit to Richmond, Virginia. Detail of engraving by John Chester Buttre, after a drawing by L. Hollis, published in 1866.

4 March 1861 Inauguration of Abraham Lincoln

TABLE OF CONTENTS

THE FIRST INAUGURATION OF ABRAHAM LINCOLN, MARCH 4, 1861

ABRAHAM LINCOLN'S HAT AND SUIT

Preface

To commemorate the 200th anniversary of the birth of Abraham Lincoln, the Smithsonian's National Museum of American History has produced a major exhibition that examines Abraham Lincoln's life through artifacts in our collections. While items from the collection have appeared in exhibitions and publication before, this is the first time that the Museum has displayed many of the major holdings of the Lincoln collection together at one time, and the first time that so much of our Lincoln collection has been published as a whole.

The exhibition covers each major period of Abraham Lincoln's private and public life, especially his years in Washington when he made the crucial decisions that ended slavery and preserved the nation. Included are the artifacts of Lincoln's assassination—his top hat, the prison hoods of the conspirators, and other sobering reminders of this tragic story.

The Lincoln Exhibition is made possible through the generous support of the Ford Motor Company Fund, the Richard Lounsbery Foundation, the History Channel, Elihu and Susan Rose, Brenda Kolker Pascal, and Paul L. Pascal.

The bicentennial of Lincoln's birth comes at a particularly exciting moment in the development of the National Museum of American History. The museum has completed an $85 million renovation that has transformed its interior architecture and created new opportunities for permanent and changing galleries. Along with these physical improvements, we have embarked on an intellectual transformation that emphasizes major themes of our national experience—political, military, social, economic, and cultural history. In this new setting, our exhibits and programs will continue to educate, entertain, engage, and inspire by telling the stories of America's past.

Brent D. Glass
Director, National Museum of American History

The Lincoln Collection at the Smithsonian's National Museum of American History

Sometime in 1867—the actual date is unknown—officials of the United States Patent Office delivered Abraham Lincoln's hat and his chair from Ford's Theatre to the Smithsonian Institution. The War Department had recovered these items from the presidential box shortly after Lincoln's assassination on April 14, 1865. Once the Lincoln conspirators had been tried, the War Department transferred the hat and chair to the Department of the Interior to be safely stored with other national relics that were maintained at the Patent Office. The hat, with Mary Lincoln's permission, was briefly exhibited next to a case with George Washington relics in the Patent Office building (now the home of the Smithsonian's National Portrait Gallery and Smithsonian American Art Museum).

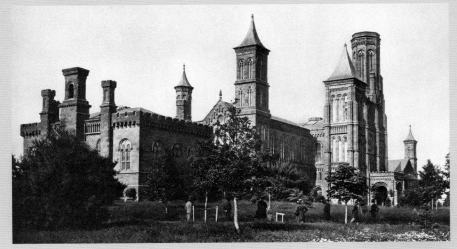

SMITHSONIAN INSTITUTION BUILDING, 1865.

Upon the arrival of the hat and chair in 1867, Secretary Joseph Henry, who had served as one of Lincoln's science advisors, ordered that the two items be immediately crated and placed in the private storage room in the basement of the Smithsonian building, also known as the Smithsonian Castle. Henry cautioned the staff not to mention the matter to any one, on account

PHOTOGRAPH OF SECRETARY JOSEPH HENRY BY MATTHEW BRADY, CIRCA 1862.

of there being so much excitement at the time. The chair would eventually be returned to the descendants of the owners of Ford's Theatre. The hat remained in storage and would not be seen by the public for the next twenty-six years until the Institution loaned it to a Washington, DC gallery.

Thus began the Smithsonian's Lincoln collection. Over the years following the hat's transfer, the Institution assembled one of the most important holdings of Lincoln artifacts. The collection grew slowly and without much curatorial direction, other than the goal of preserving anything associated with the martyred president. In 1883 the Patent Office transferred the remainder of its collection of historic relics to

PRISON HOODS WORN BY THE LINCOLN CONSPIRATORS.

the Smithsonian, which included a pair of buckskin gloves given to Lincoln days before his death. The son of sculptor Clark Mills present-ed the Institution with a life mask of Abraham Lincoln in 1889; it had been cast by his father two months before the president's death. In 1894 Mrs. William M. Hunt donated Abraham Lincoln's office suit, which Mary Lincoln had given to Hunt's husband in 1865 to use to paint a posthumous portrait of the president. The War Department trans-ferred its holdings of prison hoods, leg shackles, and keys from the Washington Arsenal and Penitentiary that were used to imprison the Lincoln conspirators in 1904.

PHOTOGRAPH OF ABRAHAM LINCOLN'S HAT AND SUIT, CIRCA 1920.

Family members, close friends, and associates of the Lincolns preserved many of the items that eventually came to the collection. The meaning of these objects varied as much as the objects themselves. Donors saved these items out of a desire to remember a friend, to help them with their loss, to honor the legacy of a great man, or to preserve a moment in history. Their motives are also part of the history of these artifacts.

Both of Lincoln's surviving great grandsons, Lincoln Isham and Robert Lincoln Beckworth, gave family heirlooms, including Abraham Lincoln's pocket watch, a presentation rifle, silver services, and Mary Lincoln's jewelry and china. Mrs. John Hay donated an inkwell that Lincoln had given to her husband. A dress that Mary Lincoln presented to her sister, Elizabeth Todd Grimsley, was acquired from Grimsley's son.

Donations often came with stories about the objects, revealing how the items were used and why they were saved. The letter that accompanied the donation of Lincoln's shawl is a good example.

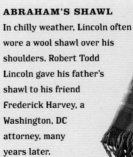

ABRAHAM'S SHAWL
In chilly weather, Lincoln often wore a wool shawl over his shoulders. Robert Todd Lincoln gave his father's shawl to his friend Frederick Harvey, a Washington, DC attorney, many years later.

My father, Frederick Loviad Harvey, attorney-at-law, lived in an era when gentlemen consorted with gentlemen—evenings spent together in book filled libraries—discussions, conversations and legal arguments over a fine wine or sherry before a blazing fire.

Among the coterie of "gentlemen" whose friendship my father treasured were Justices Van deVanter, Brandeis, Oliver Wendell Holmes of the Supreme Court, Charles Evan Hughes, Chief Justice and Henry Adams....Last in this distinguished list was Mr. Robert Todd Lincoln at whose home in Georgetown father spent many an evening. One night he returned home with a shawl over his arm saying "Mr. Lincoln just presented me with this shawl of his father, Mr. Abraham Lincoln."

The Shawl was carefully preserved. Mother kept it in a trunk in her room after father died, and so it passed to me. Again, I am so proud to have contributed some small thing to your wonderful museum.

Sincerely Abigail Harvey Wood

Mentor Graham's daughter, Lizzie Bell, provided an affidavit that accompanied the donation of an iron wedge for splitting wood with the initials "A.L." on the side. She recounted her father's relationship as teacher and friend of Abraham Lincoln when he resided in New Salem, Illinois. Bell not only identified the wedge as the one left with her father, but also recounted how it was lost for many years under the floorboards of their house.

Another note in the Smithsonian's files recounted the story behind the White House cup that Captain D. W. Taylor presented Robert Todd Lincoln in 1887.

> The cup was given to my mother by an old servant who had been in our family for nearly a decade. She stated that she had it from the wife of one of the employees at the White House, who, in closing the windows the night of the assassination, took both the cup and saucer from the window sill where he had seen the President place them after drinking his cup of coffee after dinner on that night.

The cup and letter remained in Robert Todd Lincoln's family until they were donated to the Smithsonian in 1958.

The Smithsonian Institution began to exhibit its Lincoln relics in 1884 at the Arts and Industries Building on the National Mall. By 1898 it had obtained enough material to display its Lincoln collection in a large glass case that became part of a new instillation of cases on American history. When donors presented new material curators added the items to the display. The Smithsonian did not create a special exhibition on the Lincoln until the 150th anniversary of his birth in 1959. Since then items from the collection have been exhibited in numerous exhibitions about American politics, the Civil War, and general American history at the Smithsonian and throughout the country.

While items from the collection have appeared in exhibitions and publications before, this is the first time that Smithsonian's National Museum of American History, where the collection now resides, has

NORTH HALL OF THE SMITHSONIAN ARTS AND INDUSTRIES BUILDING, 1948.
Busts of Washington and Lincoln, each in their own case, faced one another.

displayed the major holdings of the Lincoln collection together at one time. The collection currently contains material from Lincoln's early life on the frontier, his days as a lawyer and politician in Springfield, Illinois, his presidency, and his assassination. There are items from his personal life, his family and close associates, and objects that document major milestones in his political career. As a whole, the collection presents a personal and intimate look at Lincoln. It reminds us that Abraham Lincoln, whose story has become so mythic, was a real person. Through these objects, we can better understand both an individual and a time that has shaped our nation and its future.

ABRAHAM LINCOLN, AGE 54

Photograph by Alexander Gardner in Washington, DC, 1863, probably taken eleven days before Lincoln delivered the Gettysburg Address.

Introduction

Throughout his life, Abraham Lincoln wondered if he would leave his mark on history. Today, two hundred years after his birth, people around the world still find inspiration in his story.

Like no other American, his life is entwined with the history and culture of the nation. Lincoln's rise from poverty to the presidency has inspired others to believe in the promise of opportunity; his triumph in preserving a democratic nation is one of our greatest triumphs; and his death is our American tragedy.

This unschooled politician from the western frontier guided our nation through its greatest crisis and helped define America's future through the force of his leadership and intellect. Abraham Lincoln has encouraged generations with his generous spirit and his willingness to give his life so that "government of the people, by the people, for the people, shall not perish from the earth."

Early Life

ABRAHAM LINCOLN, AGE 37
Daguerreotype believed to have been made by N. H. Shepard in Springfield, Illinois. The daguerreotype is the first known portrait of Abraham Lincoln, taken when he was elected to the U.S. House of Representatives in 1846.

Abraham Lincoln was born on February 12, 1809, in an isolated, one-room log cabin near Hodgenville, Kentucky. His early life on the frontier included close family ties, hardships, losses, and few opportunities for formal education. Lincoln's drive to escape this life and leave his mark on history led him out of the frontier and onto the national stage of American politics.

THOMAS—LINCOLN'S FATHER
Thomas Lincoln, Abraham's father, was also a child of the frontier. He had seen his own father killed by Shawnee Indians. Largely a subsistence farmer, Thomas moved his family from Kentucky to Indiana and eventually to Illinois in search of better prospects. Thomas' relationship with his son grew increasingly strained as Abraham matured. By the end of Thomas' life, they no longer spoke.

"IT IS GREAT FOLLY TO ATTEMPT TO MAKE ANYTHING OUT OF MY EARLY LIFE. IT CAN ALL BE CONDENSED TO A SINGLE SENTENCE, AND THAT SENTENCE YOU WILL FIND IN GRAY'S ELEGY: 'THE SHORT AND SIMPLE ANNALS OF THE POOR.'" *A. Lincoln* 1860

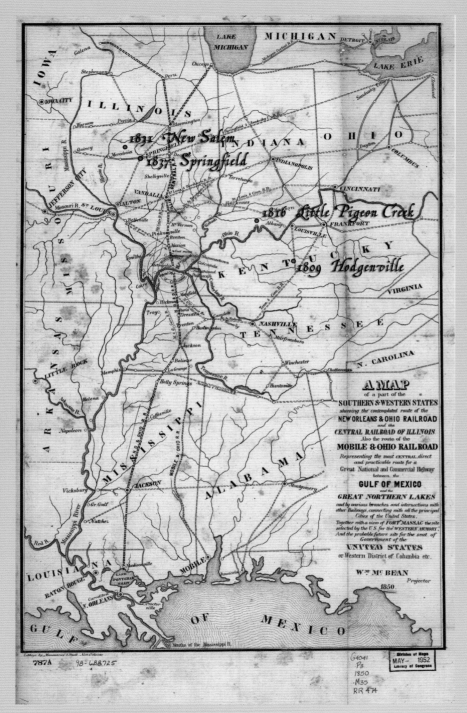

ANNOTATED RAILROAD MAP, 1850

"MY CHILDHOOD-HOME I SEE AGAIN, AND GLADDEN WITH THE VIEW; AND STILL AS MEM'RIES CROWD MY BRAIN, THERE'S SADNESS IN IT TOO.

O MEMORY! THOU MID-WAY WORLD TWIXT EARTH AND PARADISE, WHERE THINGS DECAYED, AND LOVED ONES LOST IN DREAMY SHADOWS RISE....

I RANGE THE FIELDS WITH PENSIVE TREAD, AND PACE THE HOLLOW ROOMS; AND FEEL (COMPANIONS OF THE DEAD) I'M LIVING IN THE TOMBS." *A. Lincoln*

Abraham Lincoln wrote this poem in 1844, after visiting his childhood home in Indiana.

SARAH—LINCOLN'S STEPMOTHER

Abraham Lincoln's family moved from Kentucky to Little Pigeon Creek, Indiana, in 1816. Two years later, his mother, Nancy Lincoln, died of milk-sickness, an illness caused by drinking contaminated milk. The next year, Thomas married Sarah Bush Johnson, a widow with three children. The Lincoln family now included Thomas and Sarah, her children, Abraham, his sister Sarah, and a cousin, Dennis Hanks.

Sarah brought stability to the family. Although illiterate herself, she encouraged the children's education and supported Abraham in his love of books and learning.

For most children on the frontier hard manual labor was the norm. As a young boy Lincoln was expected to help clear land, build fences, plant and tend crops, and care for livestock. As he grew older, his father regularly hired him out to other farmers—the wages Lincoln brought home helped to keep the family afloat. At age 21, he left his father's home to seek a life away from farming.

Lincoln's rural upbringing remained part of his identity as he pursued a new life as a gentleman lawyer and political leader.

"IT IS VERY STRANGE THAT I, A BOY BROUGHT UP IN THE WOODS, SEEING AS IT WERE BUT LITTLE OF THE WORLD, SHOULD BE DRIFTED INTO THE VERY APEX OF THIS GREAT EVENT."

A. Lincoln on the Civil War, July 1864

INITIALED IN IRON

In 1885 workers found this wedge during renovations to a house that once belonged to Mentor Graham in New Salem, Illinois. Graham was a friend of Abraham Lincoln's, and Lincoln gave him the wedge as a token of friendship when he left New Salem to begin his career as a lawyer in Springfield. The initials "A L" appear on one side of the wedge. John Spears, a neighbor, recalled the day Lincoln went to a blacksmith shop and asked to have his initials cut into the wedge. The blacksmith hesitated, claiming he was "no scholar." Lincoln borrowed the tools and marked the wedge himself.

LINCOLN'S WEDGE
In the early 1830s Lincoln used this iron wedge to split wood in New Salem, Illinois. His initials are chiseled on one side.

FENCE RAIL POLITICS

In May 1860 Illinois Republicans met to decide their presidential nominee. Lincoln's supporters staged a demonstration in the meeting hall, which they capped off with John Hanks carrying in two fence rails split by Lincoln and Hanks. Suspended from the rails was a banner that read: "Abraham Lincoln the Rail Candidate for President in 1860."

The delegates wildly cheered the theatrics, and Lincoln handily won the nomination. One observer noted, "That banner was to be the 'Battle flag' in the coming contest between 'labor free' and 'labor slave,' between democracy and aristocracy." In that moment, Abraham Lincoln came to symbolize the self-made frontiersman and represent honest, enterprising labor.

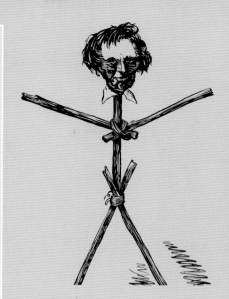

THE BACKWOODS CANDIDATE
The imagery of the railsplitter helped to define Lincoln as a man of the people, but critics also used it to characterize him as a simple-minded backwoodsman unqualified for high office. Cartoon by Frank Bellew, 1860.

"THE GENUINE RAIL"

The affidavit reads, "This is to certify that this is one of the genuine rails split by A Lincoln and myself in 1829 and 30." John Hanks sold pieces of other fence rails to Lincoln supporters during the presidential campaign of 1860. This piece, cut from a larger rail, was later sold to raise money for Union soldiers. Piece of fence rail with an affidavit from John Hanks, Lincoln's cousin.

OUR RAILSPLITTER
Illinois politician Richard J. Oglesby first crafted the image of Lincoln as "the railsplitter." He sought to find "one thing in Mr. Lincoln's unsuccessful career as a worker that could be made an emblem ... [to] make enthusiastic the working people." A life-size oil portrait painted for Lincoln's presidential campaign in 1860.

LAWYER

"Profession, a Lawyer."

—Abraham Lincoln's entry in the *Dictionary of Congress*, 1848

In 1834, when Lincoln was twenty-five years old and living in New Salem, Illinois, he ran for and won a seat in the Illinois legislature. After the victory, he borrowed money to purchase his first suit and took up the study of law.

Lincoln had been a farmer, laborer, raftsman, store clerk, postman, and surveyor. But with his love of debating, storytelling, and reading, he found his calling in law and politics. He practiced law and remained active in politics for the rest of his life, serving four terms in the Illinois state legislature and one term in the US House of Representatives.

WILLIAM HERNDON, LAW PARTNER

As a young lawyer, Lincoln served as a junior partner in two firms. In 1844 he was ready to take the lead. He invited a young attorney, William Henry Herndon, to form a partnership. The Lincoln and Herndon partnership in Springfield, Illinois, lasted the rest of Lincoln's life.

LINCOLN IN COURT

Abraham Lincoln learned the law by borrowing books and training informally with practicing lawyers. He was admitted to the Illinois bar in 1836 and practiced law there for twenty-five years.

Lincoln strove to be what he considered an honest lawyer, one who represented the interests of his client, charged fair fees, and never stirred up unnecessary litigation. His law practice was similar to many other small town lawyers of the time who tried to serve the varied needs of their communities. The majority of Lincoln's work involved settling debts and business disputes, negotiating contracts and divorces, and defending some criminal cases. An occasional case took him to a federal court or the Illinois Supreme Court. While his biggest single client was the Illinois Central Railroad, he would just as likely oppose railroads in the courtroom as represent them. His law practice allowed him to live a comfortable middle-class life and to pursue his political interests. Photograph by Abraham Byers, May 7, 1858.

"YOU SHOULD LEARN MORE THAN I EVER DID, BUT YOU WILL NEVER HAVE SO GOOD A TIME."

A. Lincoln on learning that his son Robert planned to attend Harvard Law School

WHERE LINCOLN WORKED

Senator Everett Dirksen of Illinois purchased this desk for ten dollars. As Republican minority leader, Dirksen played a crucial role in helping to write and pass civil rights legislation of the 1960s. It is likely that some of this work was done on this desk. One can imagine Dirksen invoking the memory of Lincoln as he wrote.

After the senator's death, Mrs. Dirksen donated the desk to the Smithsonian in 1970. "I remember Everett's excitement when he learned that the very desk Lincoln used was still stored in the courthouse basement … with great reverence he placed his Lincoln desk in our upstairs bedroom. It was his pride and joy. When he was at home in Pekin, instead of Washington, he would take his work upstairs to his Lincoln desk every evening after supper, rather than working in his downstairs study."

THE MUD CIRCUIT DESK

Many of Lincoln's cases were in central Illinois' Fourteenth Circuit, known as the "mud circuit" for its poor roads. Stopping at county seats, the circuit judge and a traveling band of lawyers would quickly handle pending cases and disputes and then move on to the next town. Lincoln loved the camaraderie and courtroom sparring of the circuit.

This wooden desk is from the courthouse in Pekin, Illinois. Lincoln and his fellow circuit lawyers shared the work space as they prepared their cases. Most of the desk is not original; only the pierced gallery railing survives from Lincoln's time.

LINCOLN'S WATCH

Lincoln's English gold watch and chain were purchased in the 1850s from George Chatterton, a Springfield, Illinois jeweler. Though he was not an outwardly vain man, Lincoln's fine gold watch was a conspicuous symbol of his success.

Like many people of his era, Lincoln believed deeply in the value of personal initiative, inventiveness, and scientific and technological change. During his time in the Illinois legislature, he supported government-sponsored internal improvements, canal building, and river commerce.

Lincoln's mechanical and scientific interests began with his training as a surveyor in New Salem, Illinois and continued throughout his life. In 1848 he decided to try his own hand at developing an invention to lift boats grounded in shallow water.

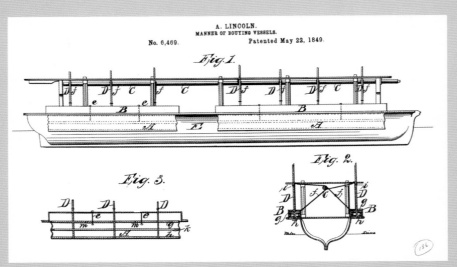

PATENT PAPERS
Patent model drawing from patent papers.

BACKGROUND GRAPHIC:
Patent papers

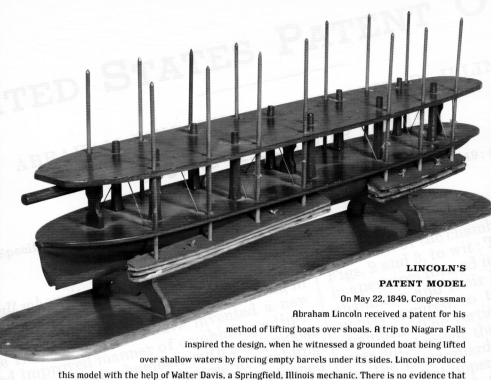

"Occasionally [Lincoln] would bring the model in the office, and while whittling on it would descant on its merits and the revolution it was destined to work in steamboat navigation. Although I regarded the thing as impracticable I said nothing, probably out of respect for Lincoln's well-known reputation as a boatman. The model was sent or taken by him to Washington, where a patent was issued, but the invention was never applied to any vessel, so far as I ever learned, and the threatened revolution in steamboat architecture and navigation never came to pass."

WILLIAM H. HERNDON, *HERNDON'S LINCOLN: THE TRUE STORY OF A GREAT LIFE,* 1888

Presidential Campaign

ABRAHAM LINCOLN, AGE 51
Photograph taken during the 1860 presidential campaign by Preston Butler, Springfield, Illinois.

Slavery and its expansion into the western territories were the central issues of the election. Like many Northerners, Lincoln believed that if slavery were permitted in the west, it would eventually move north. Southern slaveholders thought that banning slavery in the territories would lead to its abolition across the country. This debate fractured the old political parties into regional factions and led to the most critical election in the nation's history.

"'A HOUSE DIVIDED AGAINST ITSELF CAN NOT STAND.' I BELIEVE THIS GOVERNMENT CANNOT ENDURE, PERMANENTLY HALF SLAVE AND HALF FREE. I DO NOT EXPECT THE UNION TO BE DISSOLVED—I DO NOT EXPECT THE HOUSE TO FALL—BUT I DO EXPECT IT WILL CEASE TO BE DIVIDED. IT WILL BECOME ALL ONE THING, OR ALL THE OTHER." *A. Lincoln* June 16, 1858

PROMINENT CANDIDATES FOR THE REPUBLICAN PRESIDENTIAL NOMINATION AT CHICAGO.—[FROM PHOTOGRAPHS BY BRADY.]

CANDIDATE LINCOLN

By the time of the 1860 Republican Party presidential nominating convention, Lincoln had long been active in Illinois and national politics. In addition to serving in the state legislature and US House of Representatives, in the 1850s he helped establish the Republican Party. He gained national attention for his well-publicized debates with Stephen Douglas in the 1858 Illinois senate campaign and for his 1860 speech at New York City's Cooper Union.

As this print illustrates, Abraham Lincoln was one of the many candidates competing to head the Republican Party ticket, and certainly not the most prominent one. Senator William H. Seward of New York was the front-runner among Republicans, but his supporters could not put together a majority of delegates. On the third ballot Lincoln emerged as the convention's compromise candidate.

Harper's Weekly, May 12, 1860.

THE ORIGINAL CASTS

In 1886 Volk's son sold the casts of Lincoln's face and hands to a group who proposed having the sculptor Augustus Saint-Gaudens make a limited set of replicas.

In 1888 the thirty-three supporters of this project presented Volk's personal copies of the life mask and hands, along with bronze replicas produced by Saint-Gaudens, to the US government for preservation. The donation was made on the condition that "the original plaster casts should never be tampered with." Any future casts could only be made from the bronze replicas.

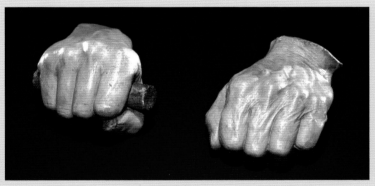

CASTS OF LINCOLN

Chicago artist Leonard Volk produced this plaster life mask of Abraham Lincoln in April 1860. Volk made the casts of Lincoln's hands on May 20, two days after the Republican Party nominated him for the presidency. Lincoln's right hand was still swollen from shaking hands with supporters. To steady his hand in the mold, Lincoln went out to the woodshed and cut off a piece of broom handle. Volk later placed the piece of handle in the cast displayed here.

"THERE IS THE ANIMAL HIMSELF."

A. Lincoln on first seeing the life mask in Volk's studio

Like other presidential candidates of his time, Lincoln stayed home in Springfield, Illinois, while party leaders spoke on his behalf. Political clubs decorated their headquarters with fence rails and organized massive rallies throughout the North. The platform of the Republican Party called for a prohibition of the extension of slavery, defense of the Union, and government support of roads, canals, and other internal improvements.

TORCHLIGHT PARADE
Grand torchlight parade for Abraham Lincoln in New York City, October 3, 1860. Published in *Frank Leslie's Illustrated Newspaper*, October 13, 1860.

"It is said that this was the most stupendous pageant ever witnessed in New York....Each special organization bore its own banner or devise, or both—each company had its own peculiar motto, its own leader, its own band of music, and urged to jubilant demonstrations by its own innate enthusiasm."

FRANK LESLIE'S ILLUSTRATED NEWSPAPER, OCTOBER 13, 1860

IN THE CITY OF NEW YORK, ON WEDNESDAY EVENING, OCTOBER 3RD, 1860—THE SECOND DIVISION OF THE PROCESSION
LAND ENOUGH TO GIVE US EACH A FARM," PASSING ROUND THE PARK AND UP THROUGH CITY HALL SQUARE.—SEE P.

HURRAH for LINCOLN

CAMPAIGN TORCHES, 1860

Lincoln supporters organized torchlight parades
throughout the North during the 1860 campaign.

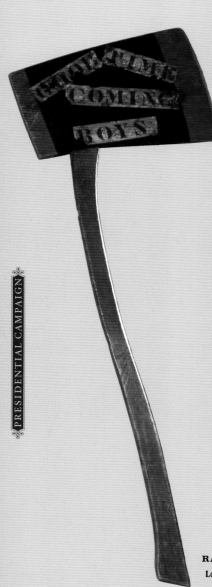

PARADE TRANSPARENCY

This three-sided transparency was originally illumi-
nated from inside by a small oil lamp and carried in
campaign parades.

RAILSPLITTER'S CAMPAIGN PARADE AX

Local Republican Party club members carried this
wooden parade ax, and others like it, as they
paraded through the streets of northern towns
rallying support for Old Abe the railsplitter.

MARCHING FOR LINCOLN
"The Electoral Agents of Abraham Lincoln."
Published in *The Illustrated News of the World*, December 8, 1860.

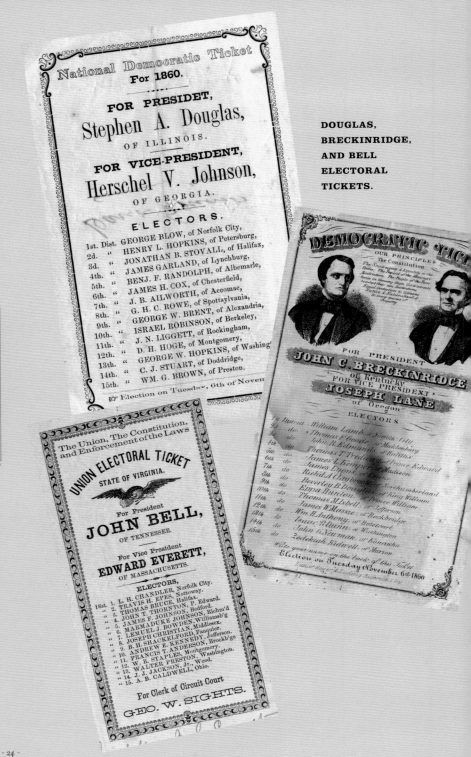

DOUGLAS,
BRECKINRIDGE,
AND BELL
ELECTORAL
TICKETS.

A Fractured Election

In 1860 the Democratic Party split over the issue of slavery. Northern Democrats nominated Stephen Douglas for president. His platform called for residents of each territory to decide whether to permit slavery. Southern Democrats nominated John C. Breckinridge and called for slavery's expansion into the west. Members of the new Constitutional Party tried to avoid taking any controversial positions, and simply promised to maintain the Constitution, the Union, and the laws. Their nominee was John Bell. Lincoln, the Republican candidate, won the election by carrying the North but received less than 40 percent of the national popular vote.

"The News of Lincoln's Election"

*"Yesterday, November the 7th, will long be a memorable
day in Charleston. The tea has been thrown
overboard—the revolution of 1860 has been initiated."*

MERCURY NEWSPAPER,
CHARLESTON, SOUTH CAROLINA, NOVEMBER 8, 1860.

Electio.

States/Territories	Electoral Votes
WASHINGTON TERR	
OREGON	3
UNORG TERR	
MINN	4
WIS	5
NEBRASKA TERR	
IOWA	4
UTAH TERR	
ILI	11
CALIF	4
KANSAS TERR	
MO	9
NEW MEXICO TERR	
UNORG TERR	
ARK	4
MIS	7
TEXAS	4
LA	6

Territories

CANDIDATES	POPULAR VOTES
LINCOLN	1,866,452
DOUGLAS	1,375,157
BRECKINRIDGE	847,953
BELL	590,631

of 1860

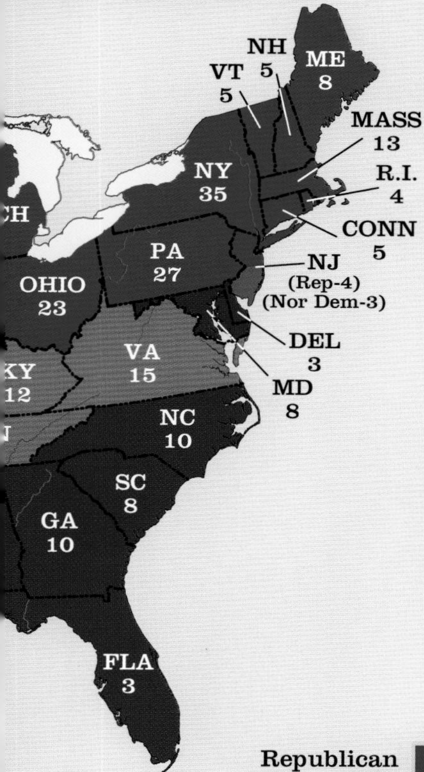

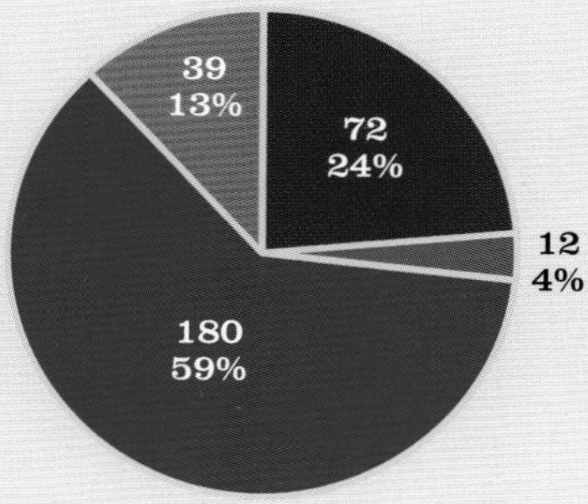

NH 5
VT 5
ME 8
MASS 13
NY 35
R.I. 4
CONN 5
PA 27
NJ (Rep-4) (Nor Dem-3)
OHIO 23
DEL 3
MD 8
VA 15
KY 12
NC 10
SC 8
GA 10
FLA 3

39
13%

72
24%

12
4%

180
59%

**ELECTORAL VOTE
TOTAL: 303**

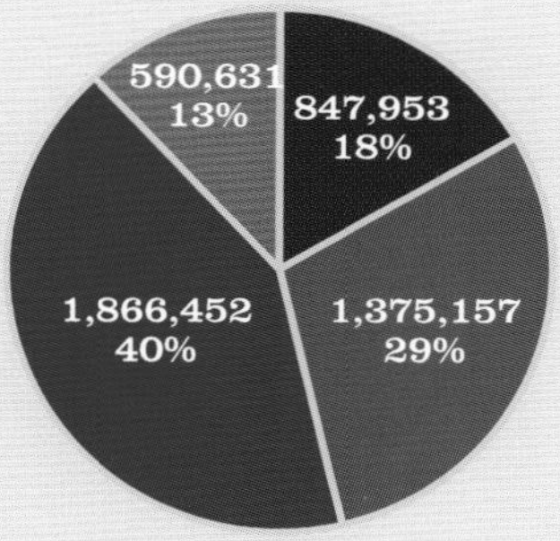

590,631
13%

847,953
18%

1,866,452
40%

1,375,157
29%

**POPULAR VOTE
TOTAL: 4,680,193**

Republican
(Lincoln)

Constitutional Union
(Bell)

Southern Democratic
(Breckinridge)

Northern Democratic
(Douglas)

ELECTORAL VOTES

180

12

72

39

The Lincoln Administration

ABRAHAM LINCOLN, AGE 52

Photograph by an unknown photographer, spring 1861. Believed to be the first image taken of Lincoln as president.

On March 4, 1861, Abraham Lincoln took the presidential oath of office. No president, before or after, entered the office with the nation in such peril. South Carolina, Mississippi, Florida, Alabama, Georgia, Louisiana, and Texas rejected the results of the presidential election and formed the Confederate States of America. Virginia, Arkansas, Tennessee, and North Carolina soon joined them.

For virtually Lincoln's entire presidency, the nation was engulfed in a brutal civil war. On inauguration day, few Americans could have predicted the depth of the conflict or its consequences.

LINCOLN INAUGURAL PARADE
Abraham Lincoln on his way to the Capitol for his inauguration. Published in *Frank Leslie's Illustrated Weekly*, March 16, 1861.

FIRST INAUGURATION

ORIGINAL PHOTOGRAPHIC PRINT OF LINCOLN'S FIRST INAUGURATION

Lincoln began his inaugural address by appealing to Southern secessionists. He promised to defend states rights and protect slavery where it existed. However, he made it clear that he would defend the Constitution and the Union. He ended his speech with a plea to find common ground. To some Northerners, his remarks seemed to be too conciliatory, but to many people in the South, they sounded like a declaration of war.

"In your hands, my dissatisfied fellow countrymen, and not in mine, is the momentous issue of civil war. The government will not assail you. You can have no conflict, without being yourselves the aggressors. You have no oath registered in Heaven to destroy the government, while I shall have the most solemn one to 'preserve, protect and defend' it.

I am loath to close. We are not enemies, but friends. We must not be enemies. Though passion may have strained, it must not break our bonds of affection. The mystic chords of memory, stretching from every battle-field, and patriot grave, to every living heart and hearthstone, all over this broad land, will yet swell the chorus of the Union, when again touched, as surely they will be, by the better angels of our nature."

A. Lincoln from the First Inaugural Address, March 4, 1861

FORT SUMTER

On the morning after his inauguration Lincoln received a report that the garrison at Fort Sumter, in the harbor of Charleston, South Carolina, would soon be forced to surrender unless resupplied. The Confederate government laid claim to the fort and looked on reinforcements or new supplies as an act of war. Surrendering the fort would only strengthen the secessionists' cause.

After much debate, Lincoln decided to send provisions but not arms. The supply ship never reached the fort. On April 12, 1861, Confederate forces responded with a thirty-four-hour bombardment that ended in the garrison's surrender. Three days later Lincoln issued a proclamation calling for 75,000 volunteers for the Union army. *Bombardment of Fort Sumter, Charleston Harbor: 12th & 13th of April, 1861.* Print published by Currier and Ives, 1861.

FORT SUMTER, CHARLESTON HARBOR.

CUMMINGS PT

12ᵗʰ & 13ᵗʰ of April, 1861.

NAST CARTOON OF INAUGURAL ADDRESS

Thomas Nast's cartoon, published in the *New York Illustrated News*, March 23, 1861, captured how different audiences received Lincoln's address.

TROOPS IN FRONT OF THE WHITE HOUSE
Cassius M. Clay Battalion defending the White House, April 1861.

"OF ALL THE TRIALS I HAVE HAD SINCE I CAME HERE, NONE BEGIN TO COMPARE WITH THOSE I HAD BETWEEN THE INAUGURATION AND THE FALL OF FORT SUMPTER [SIC]. THEY WERE SO GREAT THAT COULD I HAVE ANTICIPATED THEM, I WOULD NOT HAVE BELIEVED IT POSSIBLE TO SURVIVE THEM."

A. Lincoln July 3, 1861

THE LINCOLN FAMILY

The Lincolns moved into the White House with two small boys, William Wallace "Willie," who was ten, and Thomas "Tad," who was seven. Their oldest son, Robert Todd, was seventeen and attending college at Harvard; he later joined the Army. *Lincoln and Family,* Kurz & Allison Art Studio, Chicago, published after 1880.

At the time of the inauguration, Abraham and Mary Lincoln had been married for eighteen years. Lincoln described them as "the long and the short of it." He was six foot four; she was five foot four. He never completely shed his frontier upbringing; she was raised in a formal, well-to-do household. Each was extremely moody. He was often withdrawn; she could be explosive. Both were ambitious, and devoted to each other and their family.

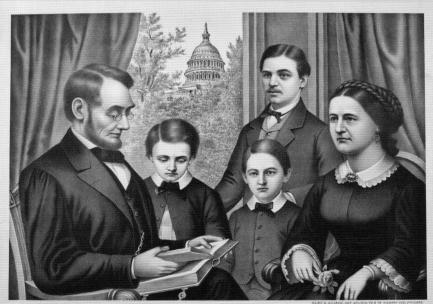

LINCOLN.   TAD.   WILLIE.   ROBERT.   MRS. LINCOLN.

LINCOLN AND FAMILY.

THE HISTORY OF THE SUIT

Lincoln's office suit was used in a preliminary study for a posthumous portrait by Boston artist William Morris Hunt. In May 1865 Mary Lincoln sent Thomas Pendel, the White House doorkeeper, to deliver the suit. Pendel, being about the same size as Lincoln, posed in the clothing for the artist. Hunt kept the suit, and in 1894 his widow donated the clothing to the Smithsonian.

The portrait was destroyed in a fire. Only Hunt's sketch, done at the time, still survives.

ABRAHAM'S OFFICE SUIT
Abraham Lincoln wore this black broadcloth coat, vest, and trousers as his office suit during his presidency. The shirt and tie are reproductions.

MARY LINCOLN AND SONS

Mary Lincoln with Willie (left) and Tad (right), taken at the Preston Butler studio, Springfield, IL, November 1860.

TAD'S WATCH

Tad Lincoln's Swiss gold watch from Tiffany and Sons of New York, mid-1860s.

MARY'S PURSE

Mary Lincoln's gold evening purse, 1863. Her name and the year are engraved inside the ring.

MARY'S DRESS

Mary Lincoln's purple velvet skirt and daytime bodice are believed to have been made by African American dressmaker Elizabeth Keckly. The first lady wore the gown during the Washington winter social season in 1861–62. Both pieces are piped with white satin, and the bodice is trimmed with mother-of-pearl buttons. The lace collar is of the period, but not original to the dress. An evening bodice, shown in the photograph opposite, was included with the ensemble.

A GIFT FROM MARY LINCOLN

After Abraham Lincoln's death, Mary went into mourning and remained in widow's clothes until her own death in 1882. She gave some of her White House finery to family members. Her cousin, Elizabeth Todd Grimsley, received this purple velvet ensemble. In 1916 Grimsley's son, John, sold the ensemble to Mrs. Julian James for the Smithsonian's new First Ladies Collection.

John Grimsley attributed this dress to a "seamstress of exceptional ability" who "made nearly all of Mrs. Lincoln's gowns." Although he mistook her name as "Ann," he most likely was referring to Elizabeth Keckly.

ELIZABETH KECKLY

Elizabeth Keckly (often spelled Keckley) was born into slavery in Dinwiddie County, Virginia. An accomplished dressmaker, she earned enough money to buy her and her son's freedom. Keckly was living in Washington, DC, when she was introduced to Mary Lincoln in 1861. Keckly became Mary's principal dressmaker, trusted confidant, and intimate friend. It was a close, complicated, unequal relationship. The women were drawn together by genuine affection and divided by class and race. Photograph of Elizabeth Keckly, 1860s.

A KEEPSAKE FROM THE LINCOLNS

Elizabeth Keckly asked Mary Lincoln for keepsakes from the president and received several items, including this inkwell. In 1874 she presented it to Reverend George Van Deurs, her minister at the Fifteenth Street Presbyterian Church in Washington, DC.

HAY AND NICOLAY

The president's private secretaries, John George Nicolay (left) and John Hay (right), began to work for Lincoln in Springfield, Illinois during the presidential campaign. They remained trusted aides and confidants throughout his presidency. Nicolay and Hay moved into the White House with the Lincoln family. Both men became devoted admirers, and fondly referred to the president as "the Tycoon."

INKWELL

Crystal and silver inkwell inscribed, "This inkstand was used by Abraham Lincoln during his presidency. John Hay."

The Civil War made it particularly important that the ceremonial functions of the administration appear dignified and competent. This public image helped calm domestic critics and reassure foreign governments, especially England and France, which were being courted by the Confederacy.

As the presidential family in a time of war and great sacrifice, the Lincolns faced the challenge of maintaining proper decorum without appearing self-indulgent. Their background made this task even more difficult, as they had to overcome eastern stereotypes of "uncultured" westerners.

THE WHITE HOUSE

The Executive Mansion needed repairs when the Lincolns took up residency. Congress provided every new administration $20,000 for renovations. Mary Lincoln took charge of the work and quickly ran up bills that exceeded the budget. Dealing with this debt became a constant strain on Mary and a source of tension between her and her husband. East Room of the White House after Mary installed new carpet and wallpaper in 1861.

SILVER SERVICE

Each of the pieces is engraved on one side with the monogram "MTL" and a crest on the other. It is likely the service was given to the first lady as a gift from the citizens of New York. Silver service made by the Gorham Silver Company.

16   [FEB. 22, 1862.]

AN IMPOSSIBLE POSITION

Mary Lincoln took her role as first lady very seriously. Some newspapers portrayed her as "the republican queen," elegant and admirable at public occasions. Others criticized her for her extravagance. Photograph of Mary Lincoln by Mathew B. Brady, January 1862.

"The people scrutinize every article that I wear with critical curiosity. The very fact of having grown up in the West, subjects me to more searching observation."

MARY LINCOLN, SUMMER 1864

THE WHITE HOUSE, WASHINGTON, WEDNESDAY EVENING, FEBRUARY 5TH.—FROM A SKETCH BY OUR SPECIAL ARTIST.—SEE PAGE 209.

GRAND PRESIDENTIAL PARTY

On February 5, 1862, Mary organized a grand evening ball that showcased many of the new renovations to the Executive Mansion. The reception was largely viewed a social triumph. Upstairs however, Willie was sick in bed. *Grand Presidential Party at the White House, February 5th,* published in *Frank Leslie's Illustrated Newspaper,* February 22, 1862.

THE LINCOLNS' LOSS

Willie Lincoln died of typhoid fever on February 20, 1862, at age eleven. The loss deeply affected both parents and cast a solemn shadow over the Lincoln White House.

Abraham Lincoln, like so many others, underestimated the cost of the war ahead. Both North and South were confident they could easily win the struggle. Each misjudged the other's determination.

The first years of the war were full of horror and frustration. Union forces appeared incapable of sustaining a successful campaign. The Confederate army, with fewer resources, repelled Union advances and maintained a threat against Washington, DC. Amid so many deaths and so little progress, many of Lincoln's closest allies questioned his ability to oversee the war.

"The Prest. is an excellent man, and in the main wise; but he lacks will and purpose, and I greatly fear he, has not the power to command."

**ATTORNEY GENERAL
EDWARD BATES, DECEMBER 31, 1861**

**ANTIETAM, MARYLAND,
SEPTEMBER 1862**

Abraham Lincoln stretched the powers of the nation's chief executive further than any previous president. He invoked the commander-in-chief clause of the Constitution to mobilize the Union army, wage war, establish a draft, and limit civil liberties such as free speech and public protest.

As much as Lincoln wished he could personally direct the troops in the field, his main task was to feed the ever-growing military demands for men and supplies. He also needed to maintain political support within the Union, which still included the five slave states of Missouri, Kentucky, West Virginia, Maryland, and Delaware.

PRINT OF LINCOLN WITH FLAG
Published in *Harper's Weekly*, October 1, 1864.

"WE ARE COMING FATHER ABRA'AM," 1862
Never before had such massive armies confronted each other with such deadly force. Mobilizing and maintaining their large armies became a central focus for both sides.

"I CONSIDER THE CENTRAL IDEA PERVADING THIS STRUGGLE IS THE NECESSITY THAT IS UPON US, OF PROVING THAT POPULAR GOVERNMENT IS NOT AN ABSURDITY. WE MUST SETTLE THIS QUESTION NOW, WHETHER IN A FREE GOVERNMENT THE MINORITY HAVE THE RIGHT TO BREAK UP THE GOVERNMENT WHENEVER THEY CHOOSE. IF WE FAIL IT WILL GO FAR TO PROVE THE INCAPABILITY OF THE PEOPLE TO GOVERN THEMSELVES."

A. Lincoln May 7, 1861

GETTYSBURG, PENNSYLVANIA, JULY 1863

PRESIDENT ABRAHAM LINCOLN, 1862

"To Finish the Work We Are In"

ABRAHAM LINCOLN, AGE 53
Photograph taken at Mathew Brady's gallery in Washington, DC, 1862.

Abraham Lincoln came to understand that to achieve a lasting peace, slavery must end. He had always opposed slavery, but never sided with abolitionists who called for its immediate end. Lincoln had sought solutions that would make slavery gradually fade from white society—limit its location, sponsor compensation programs for slave owners, and relocate freed blacks outside the country.

By mid-1862 Lincoln saw that a solution to slavery could not wait and that it had to address integrating African Americans into American society. That summer he quietly began to write the Emancipation Proclamation.

"IF SLAVERY IS NOT WRONG, NOTHING IS WRONG. I CAN NOT REMEMBER WHEN I DID NOT SO THINK, AND FEEL."

A. Lincoln April 4, 1864

Lincoln faced pressure on all sides. Radical Republicans called for immediate abolition. Proslavery Northerners and Southern unionists threatened to end their support if they were compelled to fight to end slavery. Enslaved African Americans took emancipation into their own hands by escaping across Union lines.

Lincoln drafted an executive order on slavery under his authority as commander-in-chief. On the advice of his cabinet, he waited for a Union victory before announcing his decision. On September 22, 1862, five days after Union troops won the Battle of Antietam, Lincoln issued the Emancipation Proclamation. It ordered that, as of January 1, 1863, all persons held in slavery in states still in rebellion would be "then, thenceforward, and forever free."

Although the Emancipation Proclamation did not directly free enslaved people in Union-controlled areas, it was widely understood that a Union victory would mean the end of slavery.

GOD BLESS ABRAHAM LINCOLN FOR HIS PROCLAMATION.

PAPER BANNER, CIRCA 1863

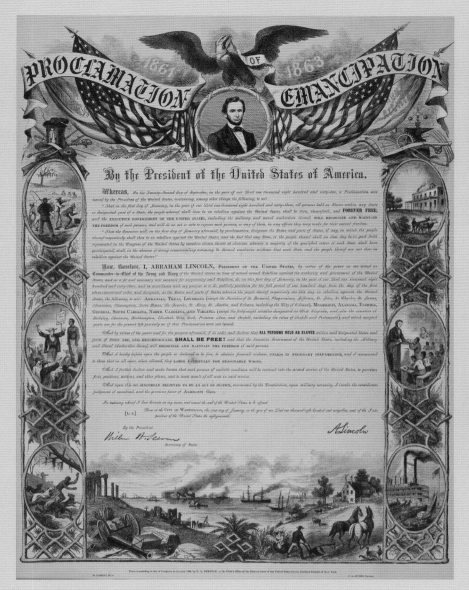

COMMEMORATIVE PRINT

Publishers throughout the North printed decorative copies of the Emancipation
Proclamation following its enactment. R. A. Dimmick published this engraving in 1864.

"THE INK-STAND WHICH HE USED AT THE TIME"

"The President came to my office every day and invariably sat at my desk.... I became much interested... with the idea that he was engaged upon something of great importance, but did not know what it was until he had finished the document and then for the first time he told me that he had been writing an order giving freedom to the slaves of the South, for the purpose of hastening the end of the war. He said he had been able to work at my desk more quietly and command his thoughts better than at the White House, where he was frequently interrupted. I still have in my possession the ink-stand which he used at the time and which you know, stood on my desk until after Lee's surrender."

MAJOR THOMAS ECKERT

FIRST READING OF THE EMANCIPATION PROCLAMATION
OF PRESIDENT LINCOLN

This painting captures the cabinet meeting on July 22, 1862, when Lincoln first revealed his intention to declare the emancipation of all persons held as slaves in rebellion states. It was Lincoln's proudest achievement, and he granted Francis Bicknell Carpenter's request to create a painting commemorating the moment. For six months Carpenter lived in the White House and used the state dining room as his studio. The original painting now hangs in the US Capitol.

TELEGRAPH OFFICE INKSTAND

This brass inkstand sat on the desk of Major Thomas Eckert in the War Department Telegraph Office. At the time, the War Department handled all of the president's telegrams, and Lincoln often stopped by to learn the latest news of the war. According to Eckert, the president composed an early draft of the Emancipation Proclamation while sitting at his desk.

"IF MY NAME EVER GOES INTO HISTORY IT WILL BE FOR THIS ACT, AND MY WHOLE SOUL IS INTO IT."

A. Lincoln January 1, 1863

The Emancipation Proclamation included a provision opening enlistment in the military to African American men. More than 185,000 black volunteers took up the call and fought to liberate those still held in slavery.

COME AND JOIN US BROTHERS.
PUBLISHED BY THE SUPERVISORY COMMITTEE FOR RECRUITING COLORED REGIMENTS
1210 CHESTNUT ST. PHILADELPHIA.

"Once let the black man get upon his person the brass letters U.S., let him get an eagle on his button, and a musket on his shoulder, and bullets in his pocket, and there is no power on the earth or under the earth which can deny that he has earned the right of citizenship in the United States."

FREDERICK DOUGLASS, AFRICAN AMERICAN ABOLITIONIST, JULY 6, 1863.

Lincoln's frustration and depression deepened as Union military defeats continued into 1863. The Union army had every advantage in resources, but failed to assemble the military leadership needed to mount a successful campaign.

Lincoln replaced generals and changed the command structure of the army several times before he finally selected Ulysses S. Grant to take command. He had gained Lincoln's confidence after winning crucial victories at Vicksburg, Mississippi, and elsewhere in the west. In Grant, Lincoln had finally found a general who would muster the full strength of the Union army against the Confederacy.

LINCOLN AND MCCLELLAN

Lincoln gave General George McClellan the task of building and training the Union army in 1861. He was a superb organizer and popular with his troops, but an ineffective battlefield commander.

Lincoln and McClellan never developed a trusting relationship. When McClellan failed to pursue the Confederate army retreating after the Battle of Antietam in 1862, Lincoln removed him from command. This photograph shows Lincoln and McClellan in the general's tent at Antietam, Maryland, about two weeks after the battle. Photograph by Alexander Gardner, October 3, 1862.

RECRUITMENT POSTER

Philadelphia's Supervisory Committee for Recruiting Colored Regiments sought to attract African American recruits with this poster in 1863.

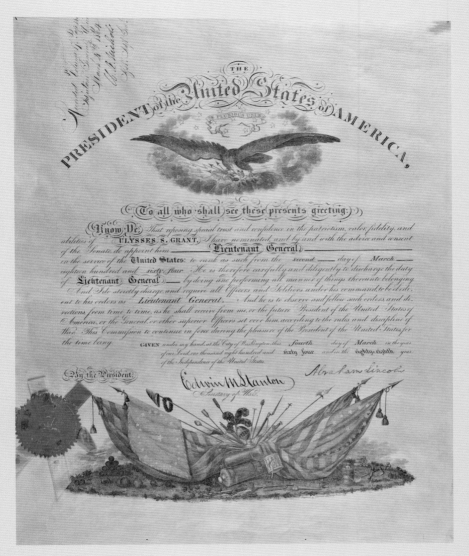

GRANT'S COMMISSION

On March 4, 1864, Lincoln signed this certificate making Ulysses S. Grant a lieutenant general, a rank previously held only by George Washington. Once in command of the Union armies, Grant undertook a relentless and bloody campaign against General Robert E. Lee's Army of Northern Virginia.

"FROM THESE HONORED DEAD WE TAKE INCREASED DEVOTION TO THAT CAUSE FOR WHICH THEY GAVE THE LAST FULL MEASURE OF DEVOTION—THAT WE HERE HIGHLY RESOLVE THAT THESE DEAD SHALL NOT HAVE DIED IN VAIN—THAT THIS NATION, UNDER GOD, SHALL HAVE A NEW BIRTH OF FREEDOM—AND THAT GOVERNMENT OF THE PEOPLE, BY THE PEOPLE, FOR THE PEOPLE, SHALL NOT PERISH FROM THE EARTH."

A. Lincoln at the dedication of the cemetery at Gettysburg, Pennsylvania, November 19, 1863

LINCOLN PRESENTING COMMISSION

Engraving of General Ulysses S. Grant receiving his appointment from President Lincoln. Published in *Harper's Weekly*, March 26, 1864.

TELEGRAPH KEYS

Lincoln visited the War Department Telegraph Office across from the White House almost every day. By reviewing military telegrams, he gained insight into the thinking of his generals and could insert himself into their decisions. The constant flow of information allowed Lincoln to follow the war as it happened and to assert his leadership over the military as no president before him. Cavalryman's Portable Telegraph Key and "Chubback" Telegraph Key.

Lincoln's early interest in technology carried over into his presidency. He took personal interest in the development of new weaponry and embraced the relatively new telegraph system to aid in managing the war. In 1863 he helped establish the National Academy of Sciences as a scientific consulting body to the government.

A GIFT WITH A PURPOSE

Designed by B. Tyler Henry, the .44-caliber, lever-action, repeating rifle fired up to seven times faster than single-shot muskets. The New Haven Arms Company presented this engraved, gold-mounted Henry rifle to Abraham Lincoln in 1862 in an effort to influence the sale of its weapons to the army. Although the federal government deemed the rifles too heavy and damage-prone for regular battlefield use and purchased very few of them, several Northern state militias acquired some at their own expense.

Lincoln had good reason to doubt his chances for re-election. No president had won a second term since Andrew Jackson in 1832.

The Democratic Party nominated General George McClellan, whom Lincoln had removed from command. McClellan ran on an anti-Lincoln and anti-Emancipation Proclamation platform and left open the possibility of a negotiated peace with the South.

As the election approached, Union triumphs on the battlefield helped propel Lincoln to victory. He declared the election results a mandate to press on for an unconditional victory and a constitutional amendment to end slavery.

LINCOLN CAMPAIGN FLAG

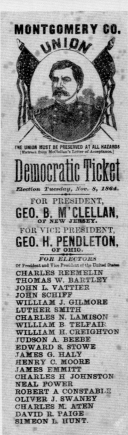

MCCLELLAN BALLOT

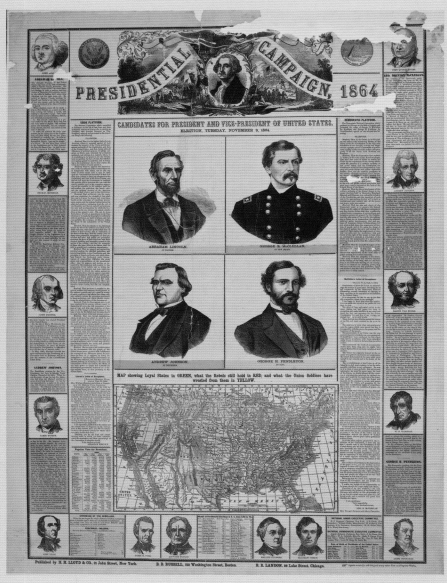

ELECTION POSTER, 1864

ELECTION OF 1864

CANDIDATES	POPULAR VOTES	ELECTORAL VOTES
ABRAHAM LINCOLN (Republican Party)	2,203,831	212
GEORGE MCCLELLAN (Democratic Party)	1,797,019	21

SECOND INAUGURATION

LINCOLN'S SECOND INAUGURAL ADDRESS

On March 4, 1865, as the war was coming to an end, Abraham Lincoln delivered his second inaugural address on the east portico of the Capitol. It was not a triumphal speech; Lincoln expressed his profound sadness at the cost of the war and his prayers for the future. Frederick Douglass noted in his diary, "The address sounded more like a sermon than a state paper." Photograph by Alexander Gardner.

"Fondly do we hope, fervently do we pray, that this mighty scourge of war may speedily pass away. Yet, if God wills that it continue until all the wealth piled by the bondsman's two hundred and fifty years of unrequited toil shall be sunk, and until every drop of blood drawn with the lash shall be paid by another drawn with the sword, as was said three thousand years ago, so still it must be said 'the judgments of the Lord are true and righteous altogether.'

With malice toward none, with charity for all, with firmness in the right as God gives us to see the right, let us strive on to finish the work we are in, to bind up the nation's wounds, to care for him who shall have borne the battle and for his widow and his orphan, to do all which may achieve and cherish a just and lasting peace among ourselves and with all nations."

A. Lincoln from the Second Inaugural Address, March 4, 1865

By late 1864 the war was coming to an end. In December General William T. Sherman completed his destructive march to the sea. Richmond, Virginia, the Confederate capital, fell early in April, and on April 9, 1865, General Robert E. Lee surrendered his army to General Ulysses S. Grant at Appomattox Court House, Virginia. Over the course of the war, some 623,000 Northern and Southern soldiers died.

SURRENDER AT APPOMATTOX
Painting by Louis Guillaume, 1867.

A FLAG OF TRUCE
This towel was used as a flag of truce by Confederate troops during General Lee's surrender. It was preserved by General George A. Custer, who was present at the surrender.

SLAVERY'S END

On January 31, 1865, Congress passed the Thirteenth Amendment to the Constitution, abolishing slavery. The measure was ratified by the states on December 6, 1865. *Harper's Weekly*, February 18, 1865.

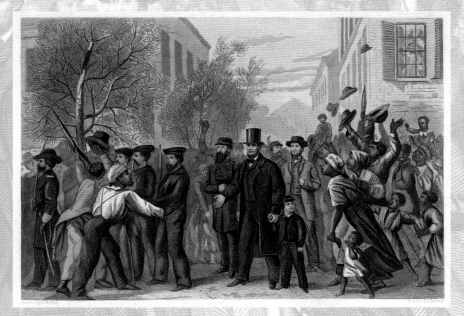

LINCOLN IN RICHMOND

On April 4, 1865, Lincoln made a triumphant visit to Richmond, Virginia. Engraving by John Chester Buttre, after a drawing by L. Hollis, published in 1866.

BACKGROUND GRAPHIC: Detail of Lincoln in Richmond.

Assassination and Mourning

ABRAHAM LINCOLN, AGE 56
One of the last known photographic
portraits of Lincoln taken by Alexander
Gardner, Washington, DC, 1865.

LINCOLN'S TOP HAT
At six feet four inches tall, Lincoln towered
over most of his contemporaries. He chose to stand out even more
by wearing high top hats. He acquired this hat from J. Y. Davis, a Washington hat maker. Lincoln had
the black silk mourning band added in remembrance of his son Willie. No one knows when he obtained
the hat, or how often he wore it. The last time he put it on was to go to Ford's Theatre on April 14, 1865.

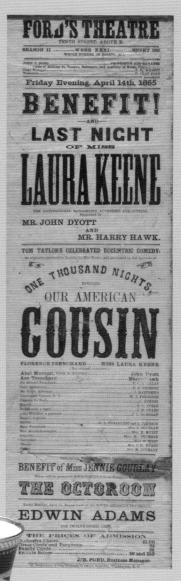

Richmond had fallen. Lee had surrendered. It was time to celebrate the victory, unify the American people, and rebuild the nation.

The deep lines etched into Lincoln's face documented the strain of so many pressures, sleepless nights, and tragedies. His astonishing resolve had sustained him through the conflict, and he looked to a future beyond the war and his presidency.

On the evening of Good Friday, April 14, 1865, Lincoln decided to spend a relaxing evening at the theater.

WHITE HOUSE COFFEE CUP
Captain D. W. Taylor presented this cup to Robert Todd Lincoln in 1887. He explained that a White House servant had seen the president leave the cup behind on a windowsill just before departing for the theater and preserved it as a relic of that tragic night.

PLAYBILL
Ford's Theatre playbill from the night Abraham Lincoln was assassinated.

Booth. Mr. Lincoln. Mrs. Lincoln. Miss Harris. Major Rathbun.

ASSASSINATION OF PRESIDENT LINCOLN IN HIS PRIVATE BOX AT FORD'S THEATRE, WASHINGTON, APRIL 14.

"During the drive he was so gay, that I said to him,

laughingly, 'Dear husband, you almost startled me by your great

cheerfulness,' he replied, 'And well I may feel so, Mary,

I consider this day, the war, has come to a close'—

and then added 'We must both, be more cheerful in the future—

between the war and the loss of our darling Willie—

we have both, been very miserable.'"

**MARY LINCOLN RECOUNTING THE CARRIAGE RIDE THEY TOOK THE
AFTERNOON BEFORE ATTENDING FORD'S THEATRE ON APRIL 14TH, 1865**

BOOTH AND LINCOLN

Actor and Confederate sympathizer John Wilkes Booth's hatred of Lincoln grew as the Confederacy's cause collapsed. On April 11, 1865, he heard Abraham Lincoln address a crowd outside the White House. Lincoln advocated extending the vote to educated African Americans and all black veterans. Booth turned to his companion Lewis Powell and exclaimed, "That means nigger citizenship. That is the last speech he will ever make."

A Maryland native, Booth was born into one of the country's leading families of actors. He was well known at Ford's Theatre. On the night of April 14, 1865 he was welcomed as he passed up the stairs to the president's box.

THE ASSASSINATION OF ABRAHAM LINCOLN

On April 14, 1865, the Lincolns and their two guests, Clara Harris and Major Henry Rathbone, arrived late to Ford's Theatre for a production of *Our American Cousin*. As the president entered the theater, the crowd wildly cheered and the orchestra played "Hail to the Chief." Lincoln set his silk hat on the floor, and the actors resumed where they had left off.

At about 10:15 pm, John Wilkes Booth entered the presidential box, pointed a derringer pistol at the back of the president's head and fired. Booth then pulled out a knife, slashed Rathbone, and jumped onto the stage declaring *"Sic semper tyrannis"*—"Thus always to tyrants"—the Virginia state motto. Despite breaking his leg as he hit the stage, Booth escaped backstage and onto a waiting horse. Published in *Frank Leslie's Illustrated Newspaper*, April 29, 1865.

> *"The shouts, groans, curses, smashing of seats,*
> *screams of women, shuffling of feet and cries of terror created*
> *a pandemonium that . . . through all the ages*
> *will stand out in my memory as the hell of hells."*

HELEN TRUMAN, AUDIENCE MEMBER

LAURA KEENE'S BLOODSTAINED CUFF

The play's leading actress, Laura Keene, rushed with water to the president's box. As she cradled the president's head, drops of his blood stained her cuff. She gave the cuff to her niece who preserved it throughout her life.

FUNERAL DRUM AND DRUMSTICKS

News of the attack on the president spread quickly as the audience rushed into the street. Maurice A. Graves of the Tenth Veteran Reserve Corps sounded the first call to arms on this drum. He later participated in the funeral events held in Washington, DC.

LINCOLN'S DEATHBED

Lincoln was carried across the street to the home of William Petersen. For nine hours he lay in a small bedroom surrounded by doctors, government officials, and family. He died at 7:22 am the next morning, April 15, 1865. Secretary of War Edwin Stanton raised his hat and declared, "Now he belongs to the ages." *Death of Lincoln*, painted and engraved by A. H. Ritchie, circa 1875.

SURGICAL INSTRUMENTS

On April 15, 1865, Surgeon General Joseph K. Barnes directed an autopsy on the body in the White House. The name of the surgeon who performed the autopsy was not recorded. The instruments he used were given to Alfred D. Wilson, a young doctor who assisted in the procedure. They remained in Wilson's family until 1935, when they were donated to the Medical Society of the County of Kings in Brooklyn, New York.

❧THE CONSPIRACY❧

John Wilkes Booth's attack on Lincoln was part of a larger plot to assassinate national leaders and throw the North into turmoil. The conspirators also planned to murder Vice President Andrew Johnson and Secretary of State William Seward. Besides Booth, eight individuals were charged. The plot was considered an act of war, so a military commission tried the accused. On June 20, 1865, the military commission found all eight suspects guilty of conspiracy to murder the president, sentencing Lewis Powell, David Herold, George Atzerodt, and Mary Surratt to be hanged and the others to prison. The conspirators sentenced to death were executed on July 7, 1865; the rest were sent to prison in Fort Jefferson, Florida.

JOHN WILKES BOOTH
Booth evaded capture for thirteen days. On April 26, 1865, Union officers located Booth and coconspirator David Herold in a tobacco barn near Port Royal, Virginia. Herold surrendered, but Booth refused to come out. A soldier fired through the boards of the building, fatally wounding Booth.

NATIONAL POLICE GAZETTE.

GEORGE W. MATSELL & CO.

NEW YORK: FOR THE WEEK ENDING APRIL 22, 1865

VOL. XX. NO. 1025.—[PRICE TEN CENTS.

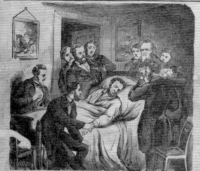

Scene at the Death-bed of the President.

Assassination of Abraham Lincoln, President of the United States.

Fight with the Assassin in Secretary Seward's Room.

Frederick Seward's Encounter with the Assassin.

The Assassination of Wm. H. Seward, Secretary of State.

John Wilkes Booth, the Assassin.

THE

ASSASSIN'S

CARNIVAL.

NATIONAL POLICE GAZETTE, 1865

1. LEWIS POWELL

Lewis Powell attacked Secretary of State William Seward at approximately the same time that Booth assaulted Lincoln. Seward was in bed recovering from a carriage accident when Powell stormed into the house. Slashing at anyone in his way, he stabbed Seward in the chest and face several times and then fled. Though severely wounded, Seward survived the attack. Powell, also known as Lewis Payne or Paine, was arrested at Mary Surratt's house and identified as the attacker.

2. DAVID HEROLD

David Herold guided Lewis Powell to the home of Secretary of State William Seward. He remained outside and left before Powell escaped. Herold later rendezvoused with Booth, and the two fled together.

3. DR. SAMUEL MUDD

During their escape, Booth and Herold stopped at Dr. Samuel Mudd's farm in southern Maryland. Mudd treated Booth's leg and allowed the two men to spend the night. He later denied knowing Booth and claimed he had learned of the assassination only after Booth had left his farm. Evidence at the trial, however, revealed that Mudd had previously met Booth. Mudd was sentenced to life imprisonment. In February 1869 President Andrew Johnson pardoned the doctor as a reward for his efforts in treating soldiers and prisoners during a yellow fever epidemic at the prison.

4. MICHAEL O'LAUGHLIN

Michael O'Laughlin was a boyhood friend of Booth and a former Confederate soldier. Evidence at the trial only linked him to the Lincoln kidnapping plot. Nonetheless, the court found him guilty of conspiracy and sentenced him to life imprisonment. O'Laughlin contracted yellow fever and died in 1867.

5. GEORGE ATZERODT

Authorities believed that George Atzerodt was given the task of murdering Vice President Andrew Johnson. Although he never attempted to carry out the attack, papers found in his room linked him to Booth and the larger conspiracy.

6. MARY SURRATT

Mary Surratt ran a Washington boardinghouse and owned a tavern outside of the city. The house was a meeting place for Booth and the other conspirators, including her son, John Surratt, Jr., who admitted being involved in an earlier plot to kidnap Lincoln. During the trial it was revealed that Booth had stored weapons and supplies at the Surratt tavern and stopped to collect the guns as he made his escape into Virginia.

7. SAMUEL ARNOLD

Documents found in Booth's hotel room revealed that Samuel Arnold had participated in the plot to kidnap Lincoln. A former Confederate soldier and a boyhood friend of Booth's, Arnold confessed his involvement in the kidnapping plot but denied any role in the assassination. The court found him guilty of conspiracy and sentenced him to life imprisonment. In March 1869 he was pardoned by President Andrew Johnson.

8. EDMAN SPANGLER

A handyman at Ford's Theatre, Edman Spangler joined Booth for a drink the afternoon of the assassination. That evening Booth asked Spangler to wait with his horse. Spangler explained he had to leave but made arrangements for another theater employee to stay. He was also accused of calling out as Booth escaped, "Don't say which way he went!" On this evidence Spangler was found guilty of conspiracy and sentenced to six years in prison. In 1869 President Andrew Johnson granted him a pardon.

Saml Arnold.
(Arraigned.)

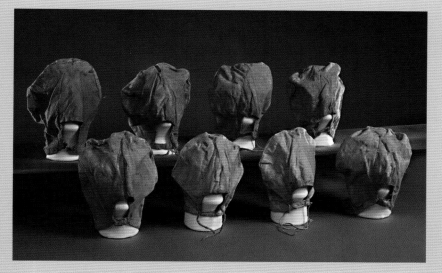

PRISON HOODS AND SHACKLES

Secretary of War Edwin Stanton ordered that the imprisoned conspirators wear hoods at all times. These canvas hoods with rope ties were made for this purpose. The accused wore the hoods in their cells and on their way to trial. In 1903 the War Department transferred the hoods, shackles, prison key, and other materials associated with the imprisonment of Lincoln's assassins to the Smithsonian. They did not record which prisoner wore which hood.

COURTROOM SKETCH

Sketch of Samuel Arnold by General Lew Wallace, one of the judges at the trial.

On April 19, 1865, an estimated 25 million Americans attended memorial services for Abraham Lincoln in Washington, DC and around the country. Lincoln's body lay in state in the US Capitol rotunda and then traveled to Springfield, Illinois on a funeral train that retraced Lincoln's route to Washington in 1861.

Newspapers publicized the train's schedule so that citizens could pay their last respects as it passed. Lincoln's casket was removed from the train for elaborate memorial services and public viewings in ten cities. On May 3, 1865, the train reached its final destination. The following day Lincoln's body was placed in its tomb in Springfield, Illinois.

FUNERAL PALL
Black silk cloth draped over Lincoln's coffin while his body lay in state in Cleveland, Ohio, on April 25, 1865. This cloth later covered the coffin of President James A. Garfield, who in 1881 became the second president to be assassinated.

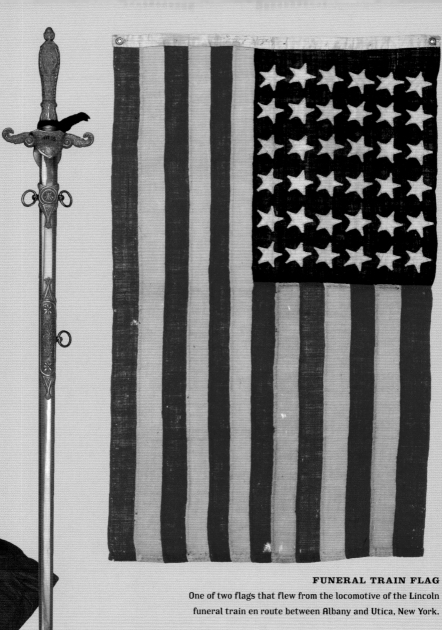

FUNERAL TRAIN FLAG
One of two flags that flew from the locomotive of the Lincoln
funeral train en route between Albany and Utica, New York.

CEREMONIAL SWORD
US Medical Staff Officer Dr. Charles Leale wore this sword while serving in
the honor guard for Lincoln's body when it lay in state at the White House
and the US Capitol. Leale was on duty at Ford's Theatre the night of the
assassination and was the first doctor to reach the dying president.

FUNERAL TRAIN

The nine-car funeral train carried three hundred guests and the casket of Abraham Lincoln back to Springfield, Illinois. The casket containing the body of Willie Lincoln, who had died three years earlier, was on the train as well. Mary Lincoln had decided that her son should also be buried in Illinois.

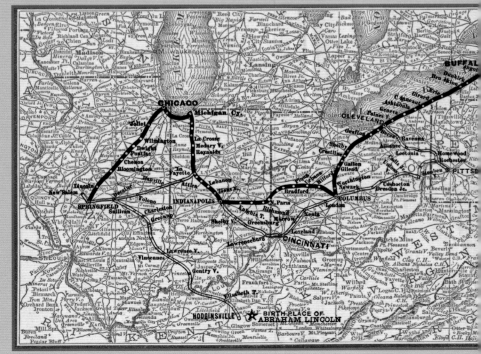

THE FUNERAL OF PRESIDENT LINCOLN, NEW YORK, APRIL 25TH 1865.
PASSING UNION SQUARE.
The magnificent Funeral Car was drawn by 16 gray horses richly caparisoned with ostrich plumes and cloth of black, trimmed with silver bullion.

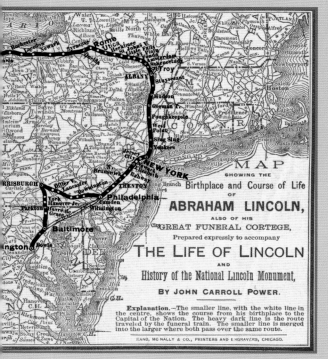

MOURNING IN NEW YORK

The funeral procession in New York City lasted four hours and included an estimated 120,000 mourners. Print published by Currier and Ives, 1865.

MAP OF THE FUNERAL TRAIN'S ROUTE

MARY LINCOLN

Mary Lincoln never overcame the tragedies she endured. She only came out of mourning on one occasion, at the request of her son Tad for one of his birthdays. The two were almost inseparable until his death in 1871. Mary died at her sister's home in Springfield, Illinois eleven years later. Photograph of Mary Lincoln, taken in 1863 and published in 1865.

MOURNING WATCH

Mary Lincoln used this black onyx lapel watch as her personal timepiece for the remainder of her life.

WRITTEN ON HIS FACE

The strain of the presidency was written on Abraham Lincoln's face. His secretary John Hay remarked on the dramatic difference in Lincoln's two life masks. He noted that the first "is a man of fifty-one, and young for his years. . . . It is a face full of life, of energy, of vivid aspiration. . . . The other is so sad and peaceful in its infinite repose . . . a look as of one on whom sorrow and care had done their worst without victory is on all the features."

MILL'S MASK OF LINCOLN

On February 11, 1865, about two months before his death, Lincoln permitted sculptor Clark Mills to make this life mask of his face. This was the second and last life mask made of Lincoln.

SCARF PIN

This gold pin with an image of Abraham Lincoln was among Mary Lincoln's possessions when she died.

ASSASSINATION AND MOURNING

"Some men stand still, amazed, when
others grow and rise to the height of the occasion,
his mind maturing and his views expanding

he tempest darkens around them;
ut few have ever grown and risen as did this man;
nder the stirring of his times. "

ROBERT DALE OWEN,
REFORMER AND INDIANA CONGRESSMAN, 1870

Further Reading

Bates, David Homer. *Lincoln in the Telegraph Office*. Fairfield & Vacaville, CA: James Stevenson Publisher, 2006.

Boritt, Gabor. *The Gettysburg Gospel: The Lincoln Speech that Nobody Knows*. New York: Simon & Schuster, 2006.

Burlingame, Michael. *The Inner World of Abraham Lincoln*. Urbana: University of Illinois Press, 1994.

Carpenter, Francis B. *The Inner life of Abraham Lincoln: Six Months in the White House*. Lincoln: University of Nebraska Press, 1995.

Carwardine, Richard. *Lincoln: A Life of Purpose and Power*. New York: Alfred A. Knopf, 2006.

Dirck, Brian R. *Lincoln the Lawyer*. Urbana: University of Illinois Press, 2007.

Donald, David Herbert. *Lincoln*. New York: Simon & Schuster, 1995.

Goodwin, Doris Kearns. *Team of Rivals: The Political Genius of Abraham Lincoln*. New York: Simon & Schuster, 2005.

Guelzo, Allen C. *Lincoln's Emancipation Proclamation: The End of Slavery in America*. New York: Simon & Schuster, 2004.

———. *Abraham Lincoln: Redeemer President*. Grand Rapids, MI.: W.B. Eerdmans, 1999.

Herndon, William Henry and Jesse William Weik. *Herndon's Life of Lincoln: the History and Personal Recollections of Abraham Lincoln*. Greenwich, CT: Fawcett Publications, 1961.

Holzer, Harold. *Lincoln at Cooper Union: The Speech that made Abraham Lincoln President*. New York: Simon & Schuster, 2004.

Holzer, Harold, Edna Greene Medford, and Frank J. Williams. *The Emancipation Proclamation: Three Views (Social, Political, Iconographic)*. Baton Rouge: Louisiana State University Press, 2006.

Jaffa, Harry V. *A New Birth of Freedom: Abraham Lincoln and the Coming of the Civil War*. Lanham, MD: Rowman & Littlefield Publishers, 2000.

Keckley, Elizabeth and Frances Smith Foster. *Behind the Scenes: Formerly a Slave, but More Recently Modiste, and a Friend to Mrs. Lincoln, Or, Thirty Years a Slave and Four Years in the White House*. Urbana: University of Illinois Press, 2001.

Kunhardt, Philip B., Philip B. Kunhardt, and Peter W. Kunhardt. *Lincoln: An Illustrated Biography*. New York: Knopf: Distributed by Random House, 1992.

Rhodehamel, John H. and Thomas F. Schwartz. *The Last Best Hope of Earth: Abraham Lincoln and the Promise of America: Catalogue of an Exhibition at the Huntington Library, October 1993 - August 1994*. San Marino, CA: Huntington Library, 1993.

Steers, Edward. *Blood on the Moon: The Assassination of Abraham Lincoln*. Lexington: University Press of Kentucky, 2001.

Wheeler, Tom. *Mr. Lincoln's T-Mails: The Untold Story of how Abraham Lincoln used the Telegraph to Win the Civil War*. New York: Collins, 2006.

White, Ronald C. *The Eloquent President: A Portrait of Lincoln through His Words*. New York: Random House, 2005.

Wills, Garry. *Lincoln at Gettysburg: The Words that Remade America*. New York: Simon & Schuster, 1992.

Acknowledgments

One of the rewards in publishing this volume is having the opportunity to thank the numerous individuals and institutions that have supported the exhibition and this companion publication.

I would like to thank Brent Glass, director, and James Gardner, associate director of the National Museum of American History, for all their continual support of this project and suggestions throughout its development. I am greatly indebted to the members of the National Museum of American History's exhibition and publication team that included: Lisa Kathleen Graddy, Nanci Edwards, Stevan Fisher, Chris Wilson, Sara Murphy, Debra Hashim, Patricia Mansfield, Beth Richwine, Sunae Park Evans, Selma Thomas, Robert Selim, Nancy Brooks, Ann Rossilli, Laura McClure and the projects interns, Joan Fragaszy, Renata Yurikov, Bethanee Bemis, and Rachel Morris. This project simply would not have happened without their insights, research, and untiring support.

There are many other members of the museum staff whose support this project relied heavily upon. At the risk of leaving someone out I would like to thank Larry Bird, Barbara Clark Smith, Hal Wallace, Jennifer L. Jones, David Miller, Kathleen Golden, Karen Harris, Carol Kregloh, Helena Wright, Joan Boudreau, Shannon Perich, Michele Delaney, Jennifer Strobel, Peter Liebhold, Janice Lilja, Bennie Brunton, Lynnetta Jones, Melinda Machado, Valeska Hilbig, Margaret Webster, Todd Cain, Michael Johnson, Omar Wynn, and Peter Albritton.

The design firm of Haley Sharpe Design, especially Bill Haley, Jan Faulkner, Kate Aitchison, Jennifer Yoshida, and Masa Shimozato, who not only provided a wonderful design for the exhibition, but also helped refine and shape the final content.

The beauty of the photography is the contribution of the Smithsonian Office of Printing and Photographic Services including Michael Barnes, John Dillaber, Harold Dorwin, Larry Gates, Eric Long, Terry McCrae, and Ricardo Vargas. I would especially like to thank Hugh Talman and Richard Strauss, for all the new photography produced for this volume, along with John Elder from The Skirball Cultural Center.

There are many individuals and institutions around the country that have generously offered their advice and opened their collections to help support this project. Edna Greene Medford; Gabor Boritt; Jason Emerson; Pamela Henson and the Smithsonian Institution Archives; Thomas Schwartz, Jennifer Ericson, Roberta Fairburn, and the Abraham Lincoln Presidential Library and Museum; Amy Elizabeth Burton and Diane Skvarla, and the Senate Curator's Office; the Surratt House Museum; the Kentucky Historical Society; Appomattox Court House National Historical Park; Hillary Crehan and the White House Historical Association; Library of Congress; Abraham Lincoln Library and Museum, Abraham Lincoln Memorial University; Chicago History Museum; Indiana Historical Society; Moorland-Spingarn Research Center, Howard University; Virginia Historical Society; Museum of Fine Arts, Boston; and University of Nebraska-Lincoln Libraries.

Special thanks to Christina Wiginton and Caroline Newman of Smithsonian Books for their wonderful work in shaping and producing this volume, and to Jody Billert of Design Literate, Inc. for this volume's engaging design.

Finally I would like to express my deepest thanks to Anne L. Pierce and Max Rubenstein, who joined me in this Lincoln pilgrimage, who traveled to more log cabins than any family should have to visit, and offered their insights and guidance along the way of this entire project.

Illustrations

All objects that appeared in the exhibition are from the collections at the National Museum of American History, Smithsonian Institution.

Front Matter
Photograph, Abraham Lincoln at Antietam, 1862, National Museum of American History

Engraving, *Abraham Lincoln Entering Richmond, April 3d, 1865*, Virginia Historical Society, Richmond, Virginia

Photograph of Lincoln's First Inauguration, gift of Capt. Montgomery Meigs, 1892

Preface
Photograph, Abraham Lincoln's suit and hat, National Museum of American History

The Lincoln Collection
Photograph, Smithsonian Institution building, Smithsonian Institution Archives

Photograph, Secretary Joseph Henry, circa 1862, Smithsonian Institution Archives

Photograph, Abraham Lincoln's hat and suit, National Museum of American History

Photograph, prison hoods, National Museum of American History

Shawl, gift of Mrs. John Shirley Wood, daughter of Frederick Harvey, 1967

Photograph, Arts and Industries Building, National Museum of American History

Section 1: Introduction
Photograph, Abraham Lincoln, 1863, Library of Congress

Section 2: Early Life
Daguerreotype of Abraham Lincoln, 1846, Library of Congress

Photograph, Thomas Lincoln, Abraham Lincoln Library and Museum of Lincoln Memorial University, Harrogate, Tennessee

Annotated Railroad map, 1850, Library of Congress

Photograph, Sarah Lincoln, Abraham Lincoln Presidential Library and Museum

Lincoln's iron wedge, gift of Henry W. Allen, 1920

Photograph, detail of initials on iron wedge, National Museum of American History

Painting, *The Railsplitter*, Chicago History Museum, P&S-1917.0015

Cartoon by Frank Bellew, National Museum of American History

Piece of fence rail and affidavit, gift of Senator Leverett Saltonstall, 1984

Photograph, Abraham Lincoln, 1858, Archives and Special Collections, University of Nebraska–Lincoln Libraries

Print, William Herndon, Library of Congress

Courthouse desk, gift of Mrs. Everett M. Dirksen, 1970

Pocket watch, gift of Lincoln Isham, great-grandson of Abraham Lincoln, 1958

Patent papers, United States Patent and Trademark Office

Patent model, transfer from the U.S. Patent Office, 1922

Section 3: Presidential campaign
Ambrotype, Abraham Lincoln, 1860, Library of Congress

Print, *Harper's Weekly*, May 12, 1860, National Museum of American History

Leonard Volk's casts, gift of the Thirty-three Subscribers, 1888

Print, *Frank Leslie's Illustrated Newspaper*, October 13, 1860, National Museum of American History

Campaign torches, 1860, gifts of George L. and Mary E. Compton, 1980; Ralph E. Becker, 1961; and Carl Haverlin, 1962.

Parade axe, gift of Ralph E. Becker, 1961

Parade transparency, gift of Mrs. Robert A. Hubbard, 1961

Print, *The Illustrated News of the World*, December 8, 1860, National Museum of American History

Douglas ticket, gift of Anthony E. Starcevic, 1960

Breckinridge ticket, gift of Ralph E. Becker, 1959

Bell ticket, gift of Ralph E. Becker, 1959

Campaign banner, gift of George L. and Mary E. Compton, 1980

Map, 1860 election results, National Museum of American History

Section 4: The Lincoln Administration
Photograph, Abraham Lincoln, 1861, Abraham Lincoln Presidential Library and Museum

Print, *Frank Leslie's Illustrated Newspaper*, March 16, 1861, Abraham Lincoln Presidential Library and Museum

Photograph of Lincoln's First Inauguration, gift of Capt. Montgomery Meigs, 1892

Cartoon, *New York Illustrated News*, March 23, 1861, National Museum of American History

Print, *Bombardment of Fort Sumter, Charleston Harbor: 12th & 13th April, 1861*, Library of Congress

Photograph, White House, National Archives (photo no. NWDNS-64-M-184)

Print, *Lincoln and Family*, National Museum of American History

Office suit, gift of Mrs. William Hunt, 1894

Oil on panel, *Abraham Lincoln*, 1865, William Morris Hunt, American, 1824-1879; 9¾ x 5¼ in., photograph © 2009, Museum of Fine Arts Boston (bequest of Miss Elizabeth S. Gregerson, 19.9)

Photograph, Mary Lincoln with Willie and Tad, Abraham Lincoln Presidential Library and Museum

Purse, gift of Lincoln Isham, great-grandson of Abraham Lincoln, 1958

Pocket watch, gift of Lincoln Isham, great-grandson of Abraham Lincoln, 1958

Dress, bequest of Mrs. Julian James, 1923

Photograph, Elizabeth Keckly, 1860s, Moorland-Spingarn Research Center, Howard University

Inkwell, gift of Captain George Van Deurs, USN, grandson of Reverend George Van Deurs, 1949

Photograph, President Lincoln with his private secretaries, Library of Congress

Inkwell, gift of Mrs. John Hay, 1912

Silver service, gift of Lincoln Isham, great-grandson of Abraham Lincoln, 1958

Photograph, East Room, the White House

Photograph, Mary Lincoln, 1862, National Museum of American History

Print, *Frank Leslie's Illustrated Newspaper*, February 22, 1862, National Museum of American History

Photograph, Willie Lincoln, Abraham Lincoln Presidential Library and Museum

Photograph, Antietam, Maryland, Library of Congress

Print, *Harper's Weekly*, October 1, 1864, National Museum of American History

Sheet music, gift of King S. Levin, 1980

Photograph, Gettysburg, Pennsylvania, National Museum of American History

Photograph, Abraham Lincoln at Antietam, 1862, National Museum of American History

Section 5: To Finish the Work We Are In
Photograph of Abraham Lincoln, 1862, Library of Congress

Banner, gift of Dr. Clara S. Ludlow, 1911

Commemorative print, gift of Ralph E. Becker, 1959

Telegraph Office inkstand, transfer from the Library of Congress, 1962

Painting, *First Reading of the Emancipation Proclamation of President Lincoln*, 1864, U.S. Senate Collection

Recruitment Poster, National Museum of American History

Photograph, Lincoln and McClellan, 1862, Library of Congress

Ulysses S. Grant's commission, gift of Julia Dent Grant and William H. Vanderbilt, 1887

Engraving, *Harper's Weekly*, March 26, 1864, National Museum of American History

Telegraph keys, gifts of Richard Applebough and Telegraph Historical Society

Presentation Rifle, gift of Robert Lincoln Beckwith, great-grandson of Abraham Lincoln, 1963

Campaign Flag, gift of Ralph E. Becker, 1974

McClellan Ballot, gift of Ralph E. Becker, 1974

Election Poster, gift of Ralph E. Becker, 1974

Photograph, Lincoln's Second Inaugural Address, Library of Congress

Painting, *Surrender of General Lee to General Grant, April 9, 1865*, Appomattox Court House National Historical Park

Flag of Truce, bequest of Elizabeth B. Custer, 1936

Print, *Harper's Weekly*, February 18, 1865, Smithsonian Institution Libraries

Engraving, *Abraham Lincoln Entering Richmond, April 3d, 1865*, Virginia Historical Society, Richmond, Virginia

Section 6: Assassination and Mourning
Photograph, Abraham Lincoln, 1865, Library of Congress

Top hat, transfer from the War Department with permission from Mary Lincoln, 1867

Playbill, National Museum of American History

Coffee Cup, gift of Lincoln Isham, great-grandson of Abraham Lincoln, 1958

Print, *Frank Leslie's Illustrated Newspaper*, April 29, 1865, Abraham Lincoln Presidential Library and Museum

Cuff, bequest of Virginia Adler Thompson, niece of Laura Keene, 1962

Drum and Drumsticks, gift of Alice R. Graves and Mrs. Helen Graves Chambers, daughters of Maurice A. Graves, 1938

Print, *Death of Lincoln*, Library of Congress

Surgical Instruments, gift of the Medical Society of the County of Kings, 1983

Photograph, John Wilkes Booth, National Archives (photo no. NWDNS-64-M-19)

National Police Gazette, gift of Ralph E. Becker, 1961

Photograph, Lewis Powell, Library of Congress

Photograph, David Herold, Library of Congress

Photograph, Dr. Samuel Mudd, Abraham Lincoln Presidential Library and Museum

Photograph, Michael O'Laughlin, Library of Congress

Photograph, George Atzerodt, Library of Congress

Photograph, Mary Surratt, Surratt House Museum

Photograph, Samuel Arnold, Library of Congress

Photograph, Edman Spangler, Library of Congress

Sketch, Samuel Arnold wearing hood, *Indiana Historical Society*

Prison Hoods and Shackles, transfer from the War Department, 1904

Funeral Pall, gift of the Lake County Historical Society, 1962

Sword, bequest of Helen Leale Harper, Dr Charles Leale's granddaughter, 2006

Funeral Train Flag, gift of Walter McCulloch, 1926

Photograph, funeral train, Library of Congress

Map, Abraham Lincoln Presidential Library and Museum

Print, funeral procession, National Museum of American History

Photograph, Mary Lincoln, National Museum of American History

Mourning Watch, gift of Lincoln Isham, great-grandson of Abraham Lincoln, 1958

Scarf Pin, gift of Lincoln Isham, great-grandson of Abraham Lincoln, 1958

Section 7: Written On His Face
Mill's life mask, gift of Theodore Mills, the artist's son, 1889

Photo Gallery
Daguerreotype of Abraham Lincoln, 1846, Library of Congress

Photograph of Abraham Lincoln, 1854, Abraham Lincoln Presidential Library and Museum

Ambrotype, Abraham Lincoln, 1858, Archives and Special Collections, University of Nebraska–Lincoln Libraries

Ambrotype, Abraham Lincoln, 1860, Library of Congress

Photograph, Abraham Lincoln, 1861, Abraham Lincoln Presidential Library and Museum

Photograph of Abraham Lincoln, 1862, Library of Congress

Photograph, Abraham Lincoln, 1863, Library of Congress

Photograph, Abraham Lincoln, 1865, Library of Congress

PHOTO GALLERY, PAGES 86-87:

1. ABRAHAM LINCOLN, AGE 37
Detail of the first known portrait of Lincoln, taken upon his election to the US House of Representatives in 1846. Daguerreotype believed to have been made by N.H. Shepard in Springfield, Illinois.

2. ABRAHAM LINCOLN, AGE 45
Detail of photograph believed to have been made by Johan Carl Frederic. Polycarpus Von Schneidau, Chicago, Illinois, 1854.

3. ABRAHAM LINCOLN, AGE 49
Detail of ambrotype taken by Abraham Byers in Beardstown, Illinois, May 7, 1858.

4. ABRAHAM LINCOLN, AGE 51
Detail of ambrotype taken during the presidential campaign of 1860 by Preston Butler, Springfield, Illinois.

5. ABRAHAM LINCOLN, AGE 52
Photograph believed to be the first image of Lincoln taken as president, photographer unknown, spring 1861.

6. ABRAHAM LINCOLN, AGE 53
Photograph taken at Mathew Brady's gallery in Washington, DC, 1862.

7. ABRAHAM LINCOLN, AGE 54
Photograph by Alexander Gardner in Washington, DC, 1863. Probably taken eleven days before Lincoln delivered the Gettysburg Address.

8. ABRAHAM LINCOLN, AGE 56
Detail of one of the last known photographic portraits of Abraham Lincoln, taken by Alexander Gardner, Washington, DC, 1865.